MW01166461

LIVING AND WORKING TOGETHER

NEIGHBORHOODS

BOOK 2

Senior Author
Dahia Shabaka

**Published by
Metropolitan Teaching
and Learning Company**

Reginald Powe
President

Juwanda G. Ford
Managing Editor

The Office of Social Studies, under the auspices of the Division of Educational Services, selected a cadre of educators to create early elementary social studies instructional materials. All of the individuals listed in the categories below were or are teachers or administrators with the Detroit Public Schools.

Senior Author: Dahia Shabaka

Authors: Marva Brown, Barbara Calloway, Janet Fulton, Marie Harris, Annie Mae Holt, Cathy Johnson, Chaka Nantambu, Cynthia A. Spencer, Dr. Patsy Stewart, Charles W. Sumner

Project Editor: Dr. Jonella Mongo

Acknowledgments: David Adamany, Chief Executive Officer, Detroit Public Schools; Juanita Clay Chambers, Associate Superintendent, Division of Educational Services, Detroit Public Schools; Ellen Stephens, former Deputy Superintendent, Division of Educational Services, Detroit Public Schools; Kwame Kenyatta, Committee on Educational Quality

METROPOLITAN PUBLISHING STAFF

Managing Editor: Juwanda G. Ford

Production: Cheryl Hudson

Design Staff: Virginia Graziano, Carol Porteous Fall, Charles Yuen

Editorial Staff: Linda Ekblad, Elspeth Leacock, Bruce T. Paddock, Jennifer Rose

Copy Chief: Joyce M. Gaskin

Photo Research: Rory Maxwell, Robin Sand

For information regarding permission, write to the address below.

Metropolitan Teaching and Learning Company
33 Irving Place
New York, NY 10003

Printed in the United States of America
ISBN: 1-58120-831-6

CONTENTS

iii

UNIT 5 Goods and Services in the Neighborhood

UNIT 6 Technology in the Neighborhood

Reference Section

Unit 4

CELEBRATIONS FROM NEAR AND FAR

To celebrate is to praise or honor a person or an important event by doing something special. Sometimes a neighborhood will honor a person. Sometimes a whole country will mark a certain day or days. One thing is sure. No matter where you go in the world, people love to celebrate.

CELEBRATING KWANZAA

Habari gani? My name is Keisha. *Habari gani* means, "What is the news?" We greet each other with *Habari gani* each day of Kwanzaa. We celebrate Kwanzaa for seven days. Kwanzaa is based on the harvest celebrations in Africa. During Kwanzaa, we celebrate seven principles called the *Nguzo Saba*. One candle is lit each night of Kwanzaa to represent one of the seven principles.

Kwanzaa colors are black, red, and green. Black is for the African American people. Red is for the blood and struggle of African Americans. Green is for hope for a good future. We place all the Kwanzaa symbols on the table.

There is a *karamu* on the sixth night of Kwanzaa. *Karamu* means "feast." We eat all kinds of foods for the *karamu*. Relatives and friends share the *karamu* with us. **Relatives** are people who are in your family. We exchange *zawadis*, which are gifts. It is important to make *zawadis* yourself if you can.

My family follows the principles of Kwanzaa all through the year. The seven principles are:

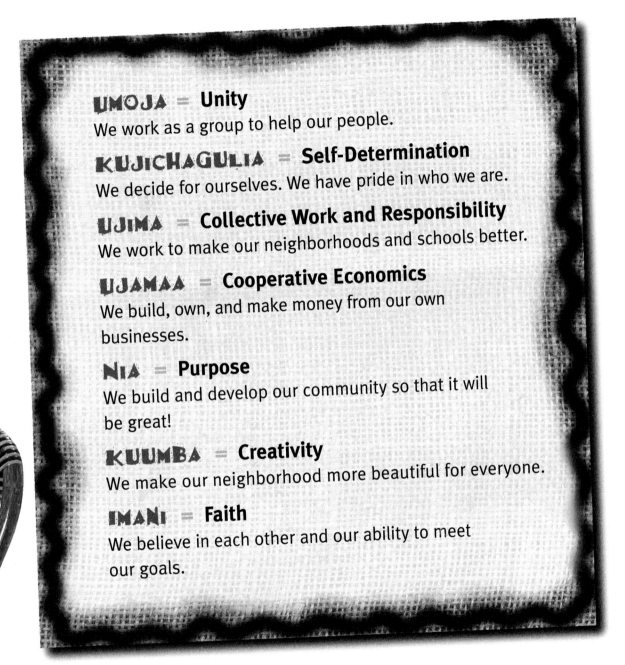

UMOJA = Unity
We work as a group to help our people.

KUJICHAGULIA = Self-Determination
We decide for ourselves. We have pride in who we are.

UJIMA = Collective Work and Responsibility
We work to make our neighborhoods and schools better.

UJAMAA = Cooperative Economics
We build, own, and make money from our own businesses.

NIA = Purpose
We build and develop our community so that it will be great!

KUUMBA = Creativity
We make our neighborhood more beautiful for everyone.

IMANI = Faith
We believe in each other and our ability to meet our goals.

1. **On what events is Kwanzaa based?**

2. **What can you do to practice the seven principles?**

Sorting Things into Groups

Every day we see lots of different things. Organizing them can help us understand them. One way to organize items is to sort them. When you **sort** things, you put them into groups of items that are alike.

Look at this drawing. The scarf is a piece of clothing. What kind of item is the kufi hat? Into what group would you sort the scarf and the kufi hat?

Fruit

Doll

Yams

Mancala Game

Look at the drawing again. Some items are food. Others are things you play with.

1 What would you put into the group "Food"?

2 What would you put into the group "Things You Play With"?

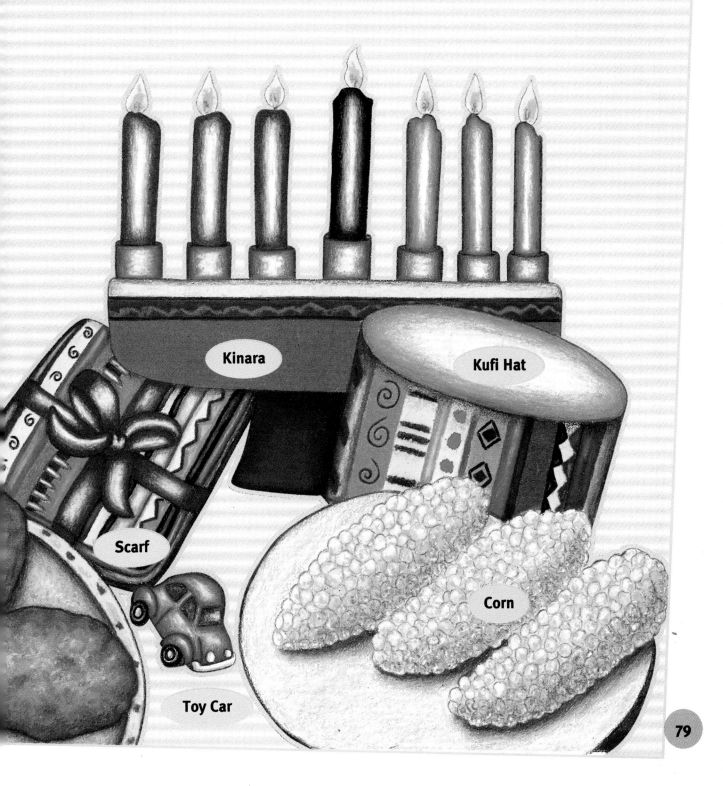

Kinara

Kufi Hat

Scarf

Corn

Toy Car

CELEBRATING CINCO DE MAYO

Hi! My name is Amy. My family comes from Mexico. We celebrate Cinco de Mayo. This holiday marks an important event in Mexican history. **History** is the story of real things that happened long ago. *Cinco de Mayo* is Spanish for "fifth of May." The holiday honors an important battle that took place on May 5, 1862.

In Mexico, Cinco de Mayo celebrates that battle. In the United States, we also celebrate our Mexican heritage on that day. The whole neighborhood celebrates. First, we have a big parade. Then, there are lots of parties and feasts.

1. **Many holidays celebrate events of the past. Do you celebrate any? Which ones?**

2. **Have you ever seen a parade? What was it for?**

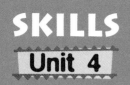
Finding the Main Idea

Most paragraphs have a main idea. The **main idea** is the most important thing a paragraph is about. Sometimes a sentence in the paragraph states the main idea. Other sentences in a paragraph tell more about the main idea.

Read this paragraph. See if you can find the main idea.

Cinco de Mayo is a Mexican holiday. The words *Cinco de Mayo* are Spanish for "fifth of May." An important battle took place in the Mexican town of Puebla on May 5, 1862. The holiday honors the events of that date. Mexicans in the United States celebrate Cinco de Mayo.

Did you find the main idea? Did you pick the first sentence? The main idea of this paragraph is "Cinco de Mayo is a Mexican holiday."

The Yam Festival is a harvest celebration in Ghana. Ghana is a country in western Africa. The Yam Festival is held in August, when the rainy season ends. That's when the crops are ripe. People celebrate the Yam Festival with a feast.

Read the paragraph above. Then answer the questions.

1 What is the main idea?

2 What is one sentence that tells more about the main idea?

3 Is the last sentence in this paragraph the main idea or does it tell more about the main idea?

LESSON 3

CELEBRATING CHINESE NEW YEAR

Hi! My name is Li. My family comes from a city in China called Hong Kong. This photo shows the parade we had for the Chinese New Year. During the Chinese New Year celebration, we give thanks for the past year. We also make wishes for the coming year. During the day there are parades, too. At night, we watch fireworks. These are all New Year's customs. **Customs** are ways a group of people does things.

On New Year's Eve, we decorate our houses. We put flowers on the tables. We put banners and kites on the walls. Some Chinese people think you can keep bad luck from passing into the new year if you clean your house very well.

1. **How does your family celebrate the New Year?**

2. **Have you ever seen fireworks? What were they for?**

Using a Calendar

A **calendar** is a chart of the year. We look on a calendar to see what today's date is. A calendar also reminds us of **special days**. Using a calendar, we can plan a vacation. We can remember when to send a special card to someone.

Look at this calendar. The letters stand for the days of the week. For example, "Su" stands for "Sunday." What do you think "Th" stands for?

JANUARY

Su	M	Tu	W	Th	F	Sa
						1
2	3	4	5	6	7	8
9	10	11	12	13	14	15
16	17	18	19	20	21	22
23	24	25	26	27	28	29
30	31					

FEBRUARY

Su	M	Tu	W	Th	F	Sa
		1	2	3	4	5
6	7	8	9	10	11	12
13	14	15	16	17	18	19
20	21	22	23	24	25	26
27	28					

MARCH

Su	M	Tu	W	Th	F	Sa
		1	2	3	4	5
6	7	8	9	10	11	12
13	14	15	16	17	18	19
20	21	22	23	24	25	26
27	28	29	30	31		

APRIL

Su	M	Tu	W	Th	F	Sa
					1	2
3	4	5	6	7	8	9
10	11	12	13	14	15	16
17	18	19	20	21	22	23
24	25	26	27	28	29	30

MAY

Su	M	Tu	W	Th	F	Sa
1	2	3	4	5	6	7
8	9	10	11	12	13	14
15	16	17	18	19	20	21
22	23	24	25	26	27	28
29	30	31				

JUNE

Su	M	Tu	W	Th	F	Sa
			1	2	3	4
5	6	7	8	9	10	11
12	13	14	15	16	17	18
19	20	21	22	23	24	25
26	27	28	29	30		

JULY

Su	M	Tu	W	Th	F	Sa
					1	2
3	4	5	6	7	8	9
10	11	12	13	14	15	16
17	18	19	20	21	22	23
24	25	26	27	28	29	30
31						

AUGUST

Su	M	Tu	W	Th	F	Sa
	1	2	3	4	5	6
7	8	9	10	11	12	13
14	15	16	17	18	19	20
21	22	23	24	25	26	27
28	29	30	31			

SEPTEMBER

Su	M	Tu	W	Th	F	Sa
				1	2	3
4	5	6	7	8	9	10
11	12	13	14	15	16	17
18	19	20	21	22	23	24
25	26	27	28	29	30	

OCTOBER

Su	M	Tu	W	Th	F	Sa
						1
2	3	4	5	6	7	8
9	10	11	12	13	14	15
16	17	18	19	20	21	22
23	24	25	26	27	28	29
30	31					

NOVEMBER

Su	M	Tu	W	Th	F	Sa
		1	2	3	4	5
6	7	8	9	10	11	12
13	14	15	16	17	18	19
20	21	22	23	24	25	26
27	28	29	30			

DECEMBER

Su	M	Tu	W	Th	F	Sa
				1	2	3
4	5	6	7	8	9	10
11	12	13	14	15	16	17
18	19	20	21	22	23	24
25	26	27	28	29	30	31

1 What is the first month of the year?

2 What month comes after August?

3 On what day of the week does December 1 fall this year?

CELEBRATING HANUKKAH

Hi! I'm Geoffrey. In December, my family and I celebrate Hanukkah. Hanukkah marks an important part of Jewish history. Over two thousand years ago, the Jewish people reopened their most important temple and relit the oil lamp in it. There was only enough oil to last one day, but the lamp burned for eight days.

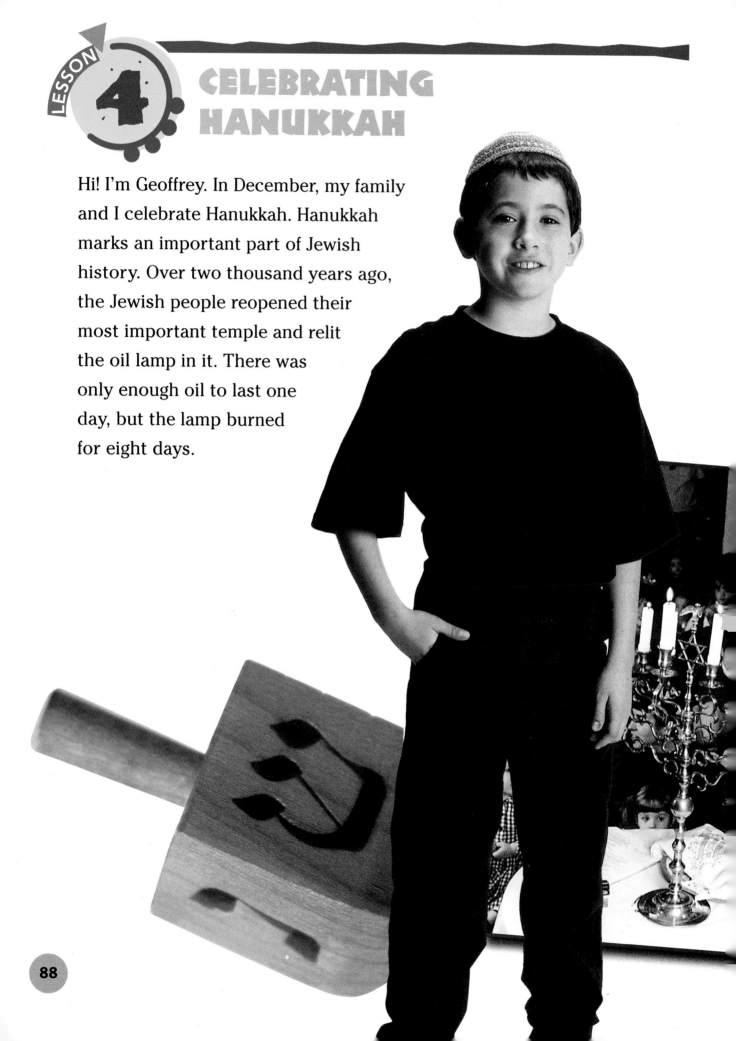

Hanukkah lasts eight nights. Each night we light one candle on the menorah. A menorah is a special Hanukkah candleholder. We also have a big dinner with traditional foods. After dinner, the children play with a square top called a dreidel.

1. On what holidays does your family eat special meals?

2. What foods do you eat at those meals?

OBSERVING RAMADAN

Hi! My name is Muhammed. My family comes from a country called Yemen. We are Muslim. That means we practice the religion of Islam. There are several things that every good Muslim must do. One of these things is to fast during Ramadan. **Fasting** means not eating. Ramadan is the ninth month of the Islamic calendar.

During the month of Ramadan, we do not eat or drink anything between sunrise and sunset. We also pray. We think about Allah, and about our ties to our family and our neighbors. After Ramadan ends, we have a feast.

1. Does your family have special days when you think about your family and your neighbors? What are they?

2. Which of the holidays that you celebrate lasts the longest? How long does it last?

Word Wrap

Use these words to complete the sentences.

history   celebrate   relatives   customs

1 _____ are ways a group of people does things.

2 When you mark a special day, you _____ it.

3 _____ is the story of real things that happened long ago.

4 The people in your family are called your _____.

Unit Wrap

People have different celebrations. Many people celebrate days that are special to them, like birthdays. Holidays are celebrated by many people at the same time. Some holidays celebrate a change in the calendar, like a new year. Other holidays celebrate the harvest. Many people celebrate freedom they won long ago.

1. **What events does your family celebrate each year?**

2. **What is your favorite holiday? Why?**

Using a Calendar

A calendar is a chart of the year. This is Denise's
calendar for the month of February.

FEBRUARY

SUN	MON	TUES	WED	THUR	FRI	SAT
AFRICAN AMERICAN HISTORY MONTH				1	2 African story hour	3
4	5	6	7	8	9 ball game	10
11	12	13	14 Valentine's Day ♥	15	16	17
18	19 Presidents' Day	20	21	22	23	24
25	26	27 Mom's birthday	28			

1 When is Mom's birthday?

2 When is Denise going to a ball game?

3 How many Saturdays are there in February?

GOODS AND SERVICES IN THE NEIGHBORHOOD

Stores in the neighborhood sell things that people need and want. The letter carrier, the firefighter, and many others do things for people in the neighborhood. People buying, selling, and helping make a neighborhood grow.

GOODS AND SERVICES, NEEDS AND WANTS

Are there stores like these in your neighborhood? Some stores sell food. Other stores sell shoes or flowers. Food, shoes, and flowers are all goods. **Goods** are things that people buy and sell. Any objects that people buy or sell are goods.

97

These firefighters do not provide goods. They offer
services to the neighborhood. A service is work that
people do for others. Firefighters put out fires. They
also teach people about fire safety rules. People in the
neighborhood are glad to have their services.

This doctor is performing a service. She is helping the child to stay healthy. Many other people in the neighborhood perform services. Teachers help children learn. Mail carriers bring people their mail. Dentists help keep people's teeth healthy.

Children can perform services, too. Delivering newspapers is a service. Helping a friend with homework is a service. Running an errand for an older person is a service, too.

Mrs. Brown is buying food. Food is a need. A **need** is something that you cannot live without. People cannot live without food. Clothing is another need. So is shelter. **Shelter** means any kind of place to live. People cannot live without food, clothing, and shelter. Of course, people need love and care, too.

Amy is buying a toy. A toy is a want. A want is a thing that someone would like to have, but does not need. Basketballs and bicycles are also wants. What are some of your wants?

1. **What kinds of goods does your family buy?**

2. **What services does your family use?**

# LESSON 2

GETTING GOODS TO THE NEIGBORHOOD

This grocery store is in a neighborhood in Detroit. The store's owner trades with people all over the world. When you trade with a friend, you might exchange baseball cards. The word "trade" has another meaning, too. Trading is buying and selling goods and services. This store buys nuts from the country of Brazil. It also buys oranges from the state of Florida. Then it sells the nuts and oranges to its customers.

How do goods get to the store? They are taken to the store by some form of transportation. Transportation means moving people and things from one place to another. Cars, trains, and trucks are forms of transportation. Airplanes and boats are forms of transportation, too. An airplane brings the nuts from Brazil to Detroit. A truck brings the oranges from Florida. All the goods are taken to a warehouse.

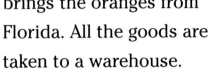

A **warehouse** is a place where people keep goods. The nuts and oranges stay in the warehouse until a store has room for them. Then a truck brings the nuts and oranges to the store.

1. Name three goods your family buys. Where do you think these goods come from?

2. How do you think the goods get to your neighborhood store?

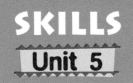

Reading Routes on a Map

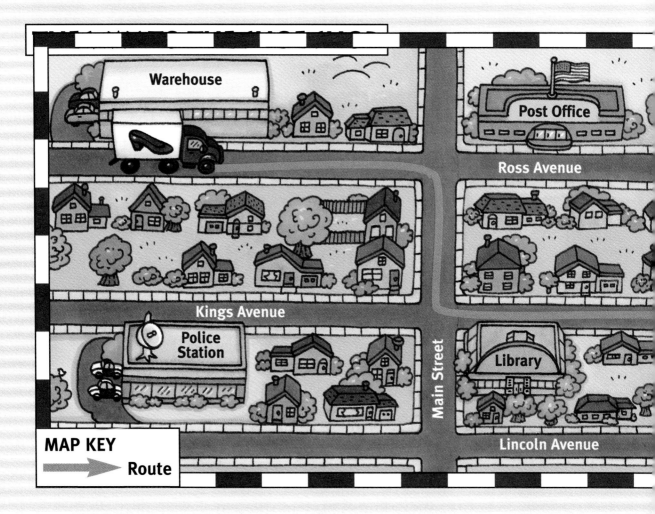

When you go from one place to another, you follow a route.
A **route** is the path you take to get somewhere.

Mr. Jackson works for a shoe company. Today he is making a
delivery. Look at the map above. It shows the route that
Mr. Jackson will drive in his truck. Where is Mr. Jackson going?

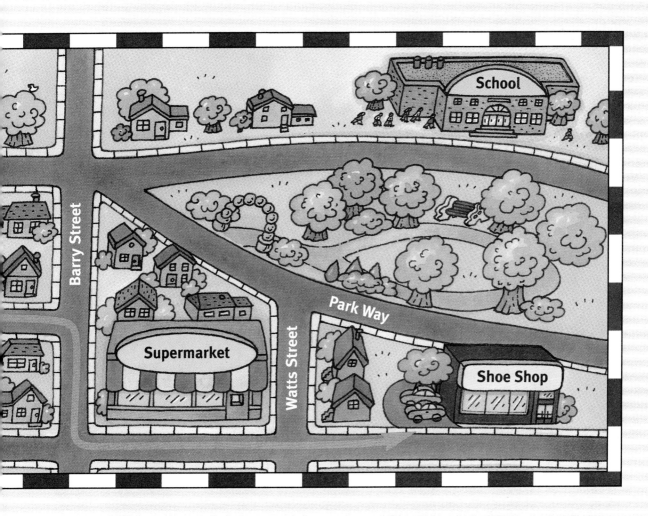

1. What building will Mr. Jackson pass on the corner of Barry Street and Lincoln Avenue?

2. Find another route that Mr. Jackson could take from the warehouse to the shoe shop.

3. Mr. Jackson takes the wrong turn and gets lost! He is in front of the school. What route should Mr. Jackson take to get to the shop now?

MAKING GOODS IN THE NEIGHBORHOOD

This child is eating a cone from the neighborhood ice-cream shop. Workers at the shop make the ice cream. Something that is made or grown is called a **product**. If products are bought and sold, they are also goods. However, something that is made or grown is always a product, even if it is never bought or sold.

This is the kitchen in the neighborhood ice-cream shop. The workers make ice cream here. First, the workers mix together milk, sugar, and sometimes fruit. Then, they freeze and stir the ice cream at the same time. Their fresh ice cream is good! Many people in the neighborhood like to eat it.

This is a neighborhood wood shop. The people in this shop make products out of wood. They make tables and chairs and shelves. They also make wooden toys for children.

This is a factory. A **factory** is a place where people make products. The people in this factory make cars.

Many people from the neighborhood work in this car factory. Some people put seats in the cars. Some people put in windows. Some people paint the cars.

1. Are any products made in your neighborhood? What are they?

2. Imagine that you could build a factory in your neighborhood. What product would you make?

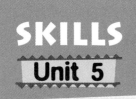

Using a Flow Chart

When we want to show something in steps, we can use a flow chart. A **flow chart** uses arrows to show the order in which events flow, or happen. It shows what happens first, what happens next, and what happens last.

Look at this flow chart. It shows how Ms. Carrera makes a cake. Can you describe the different steps?

HOW TO MAKE A CAKE

Step 1
Gather the ingredients.

Step 2
Mix the ingredients.

Step 3
Bake the cake.

Step 4
Let the cake cool.

Step 5
Ice the cake.

1 What is the first thing Ms. Carrera does to make a cake?

2 Does Ms. Carrera ice the cake before or after she bakes it?

3 What would happen if Ms. Carrera took these steps in a different order?

LESSON 4

HELPING OUR NEIGHBORHOODS GROW

There are many ways to help our neighborhoods grow. One way is to help local businesses. People in this neighborhood shop at the local hardware store.

Mr. Wilson says, "I could go down to the big mall on the highway. But if the local store has what I need, I'd rather shop here." When Mr. Wilson shops at the neighborhood store, it helps the neighborhood grow.

Children can help neighborhood businesses, too. Children buy things like snacks, toys, and books. They can buy these things at their neighborhood stores.

Kinika says, "I like these skates. I want to help stores in my neighborhood. I always shop here. Owners can keep their stores open if they make enough money. Each time I go to this store, I'm helping to keep it open."

These people like having a bank nearby. They save money in the bank. They have money in checking accounts and can write checks. When people use their neighborhood bank, the bank will be successful and will stay in the neighborhood.

Neighborhood businesses often help
to make the neighborhood better.
This building belongs to a design
company. The company supports
this Little League team. The company bought uniforms
for the team.

Neighborhood businesses help in other ways. The owner
of the bookstore gives books to the neighborhood library.
The owner of the computer store gives free computer
classes to children in the neighborhood.

This is Watsons' Diner. It is owned by the Watsons. Mr. Watson cooks the food, and Ms. Watson brings it to the customers. The Watsons live in the neighborhood. The people here like them and want them to succeed. They eat at Watsons' whenever they can. The Watsons want to help the neighborhood. Whenever they have food left over, they give it to people in the neighborhood who need it.

Ms. Garcia runs a pet shop in the neighborhood. Once a week, Ms. Garcia brings pets to the senior citizens' home. The pet visits make the people in the home happy. Ms. Garcia also helps people find lost pets, and she runs a pet club for children. She says, "I love helping the people and animals in my neighborhood!"

1. **What can you do to help businesses in your neighborhood?**

2. **Name three things a business can do to help a neighborhood.**

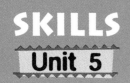

Learning About Voting

A **government** is a group of people that runs a country. The leader of the United States government is the **president**.

Who gets to be the president of the United States? The American people vote for the president. When people **vote**, they say who they want to be president. Do you know who the president of the United States is today?

In the United States, we vote for other people besides the president. States and cities also have governments. We vote for the people in those governments, too. In the United States, a citizen must be eighteen years or older to vote. By voting, we can help to choose people who will do a good job.

1 How does someone become the president of the United States?

2 How old must a citizen be to vote in the United States?

3 Who do we vote for in the United States? Use the picture on page 119 for ideas.

119

REVIEW
Unit 5

Word Wrap

Use these words to complete the sentences.

transportation   goods   service   distributor   consumer

1 _____ are things that people buy and sell.

2 A _____ is someone who buys and uses a product.

3 A _____ is someone who sells a product.

4 Moving things from one place to another is called _____.

5 A _____ is work that people do for others.

Unit Wrap

When people shop at stores in the neighborhood, the stores grow. Businesses need the people who live and work in the neighborhood. The people want to be able to get goods and services easily. When businesses and people help each other, the neighborhood grows.

1. Pretend you own a business in your neighborhood. What would you do to help the neighborhood?

2. What new businesses have come to your neighborhood? Which ones have left?

Reading Routes on a Map

A route is the path you take to get somewhere. This map shows the route Dashawn takes when he walks to school.

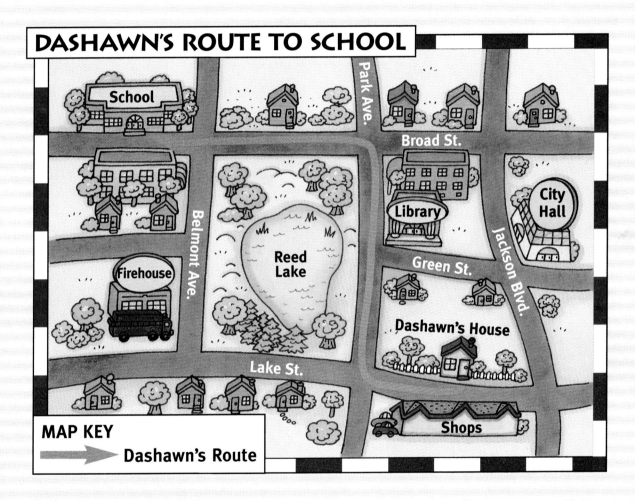

DASHAWN'S ROUTE TO SCHOOL

School · Park Ave. · Broad St. · Library · City Hall · Belmont Ave. · Reed Lake · Jackson Blvd. · Firehouse · Green St. · Dashawn's House · Lake St. · Shops

MAP KEY

→ Dashawn's Route

1. What street is the school on?

2. What building does Dashawn pass on the corner of Park Avenue and Green Street?

3. Does Dashawn walk on Jackson Boulevard? Why or why not?

4. Find another route that Dashawn could take from his house to school.

121

Unit 6

TECHNOLOGY IN THE NEIGBORHOOD

Technology is the science of machines. A computer is an example of technology. A radio, an elevator, and a bicycle are examples, too. What other examples of technology can you find in your neighborhood?

LESSON 1
TECHNOLOGY AND COMMUNICATION

When people communicate, they share ideas, thoughts, and information with each other. Talking, listening, reading, and writing are all forms of communication.

Technology can help people communicate with one another. Mr. Jeffries is using a cellular phone. A **cellular phone** is a special phone that people can carry with them anywhere.

Elise is using her computer to communicate with her friend in Africa. In a few minutes, her friend will receive a letter from Elise. How does this happen? Elise's computer is connected by a phone line to a huge network of computers called the Internet. People can send letters to each other through the Internet.

Television helps people communicate. When your grandmother was your age, she only had four or five channels to watch. When your mother was a girl, she might have watched 25 channels on cable television. Today, many people get 80 or 100 channels. Using a satellite dish, another form of technology, people can get hundreds of channels.

With more channels, there are more kinds of shows. There is more communication of thoughts and ideas.

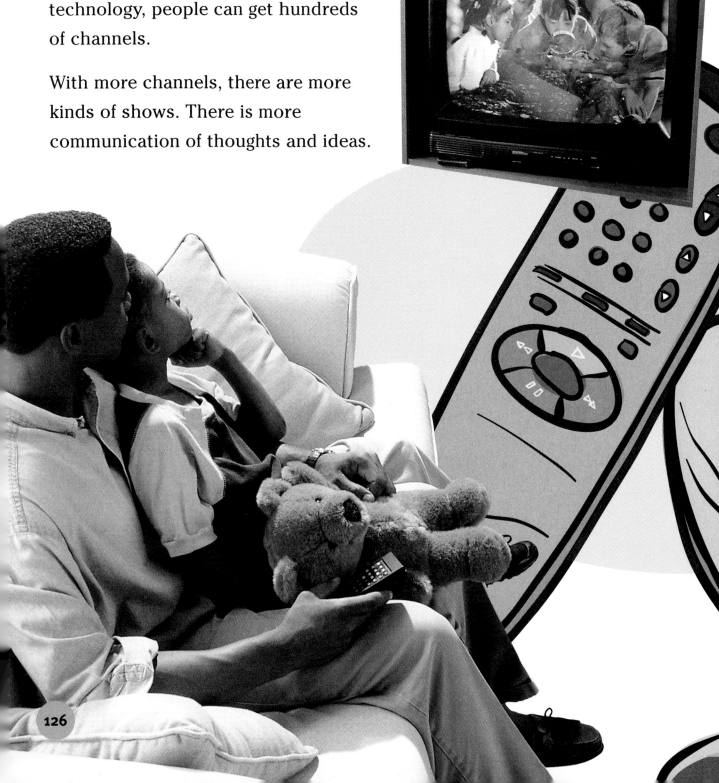

These two people are having a business meeting. They are communicating information to each other. One person is in Detroit. The other person is in Houston. A special computer program lets them see each other and hear each other. They each have a computer camera pointed at them. Can you see the camera on top of this monitor?

1. **How is a cellular phone different from an ordinary phone?**

2. **Would you like to see people when you talk to them on the phone? Why or why not?**

Reading a Political Map

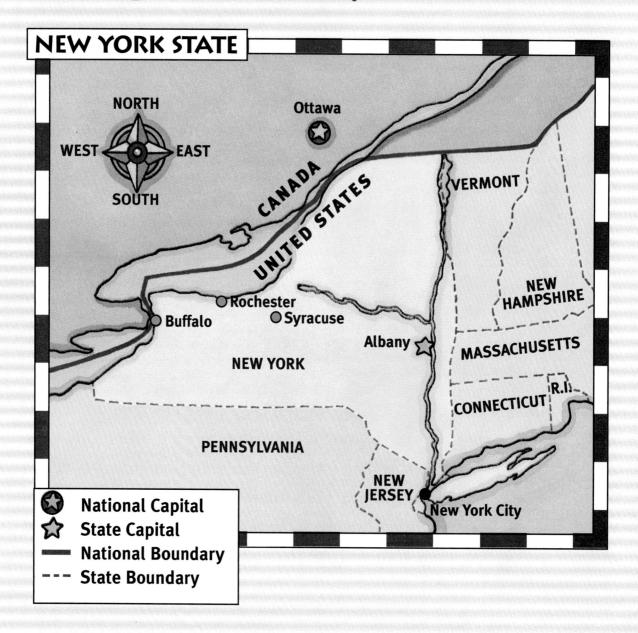

NEW YORK STATE

NORTH
WEST — EAST
SOUTH

Ottawa ⭐

CANADA

UNITED STATES

VERMONT

Rochester
Buffalo   Syracuse

Albany ☆

NEW HAMPSHIRE

MASSACHUSETTS

NEW YORK

R.I.

CONNECTICUT

PENNSYLVANIA

NEW JERSEY

New York City

- 🌟 National Capital
- ☆ State Capital
- — National Boundary
- --- State Boundary

This is a political map. A **political map** is a map that shows
information such as capital cities and boundaries. **Boundaries**
are imaginary lines between states, countries, and other
places.

Look at the map. Notice the boundary between New York and Pennsylvania. Now look at this photograph. The sign tells drivers they are crossing from New York into Pennsylvania. As you can see, there is no boundary line in real life. The line only appears on maps.

A political map also shows cities and capitals. States have capitals, and so do countries. They are usually marked with different symbols. Look at the map again. What symbol marks the capital of New York State?

1 What is the capital of Canada?

2 How many different states border New York State?

3 Imagine you are crossing the boundary from the United States into Canada. What would you see on the ground?

TECHNOLOGY AND TRANSPORTATION

Transportation is the movement of people and things from one place to another. Technology helps make transportation better, faster, and easier.

This computer is an example of transportation technology. It helps people find out what is wrong with a car.

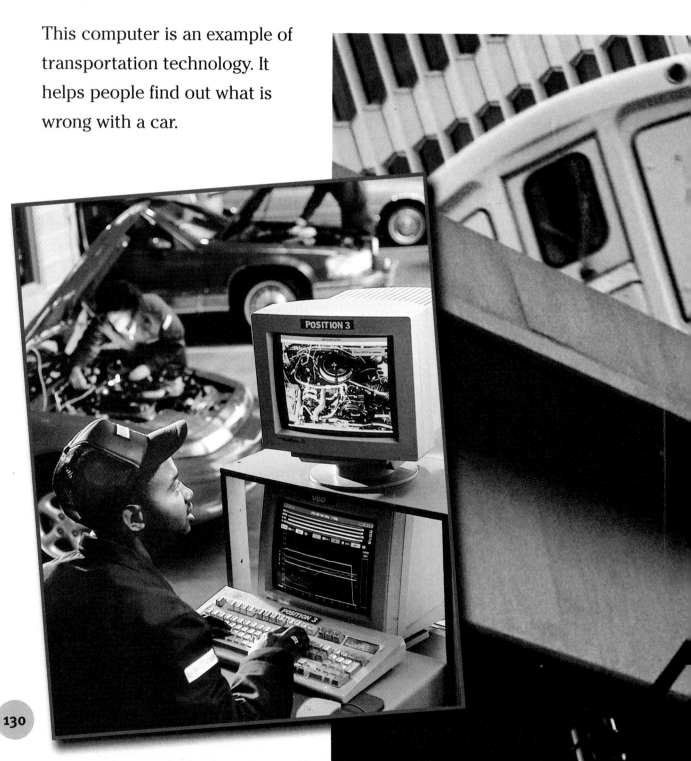

This is another example of transportation technology. It is called the Detroit People Mover. The People Mover runs on a track high above the city. The track forms a loop. The People Mover goes around the loop, moving people from one part of the city to another.

1. **How can technology help make transportation better?**

2. **How would you use technology to make transportation in your neighborhood better?**

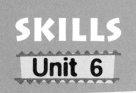

Finding Distance on a Map

There are many ways to measure distance. In a city, one way is to count blocks. A **block** is the distance from one street to the next.

Look at the map on the next page. Pretend you are on the corner of Broadway and First Avenue. Now pretend you walk to Webster Avenue. You have walked one block.

How far is it from First Avenue to Park Avenue?

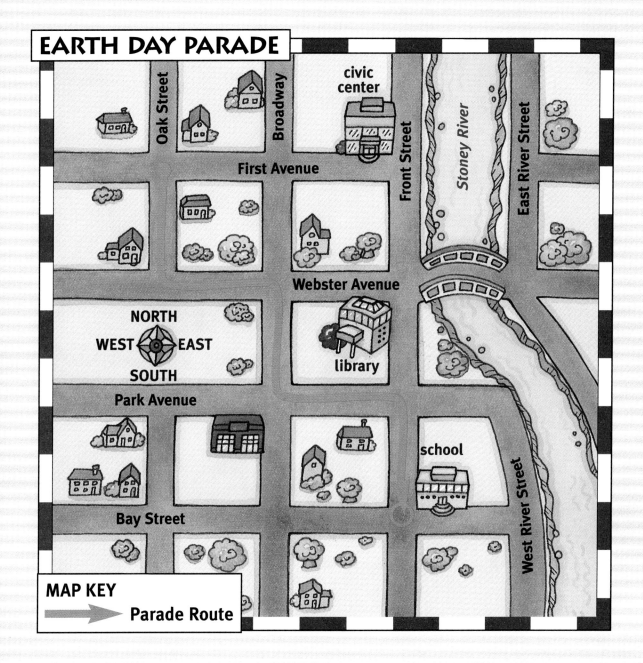

EARTH DAY PARADE

MAP KEY

Parade Route

Today there is an Earth Day parade. People from all over town will be marching from First Avenue to the school. This map shows the parade route.

1. How many blocks long is the parade route?

2. How many blocks will the parade travel on Front Street?

3. How many blocks is the civic center from the school?

TECHNOLOGY AT WORK

Many people use technology at work. The teacher in this classroom uses a computer to help her teach. The students use the computer to help them learn. The computer game is teaching them about math.

134

People who work in stores use technology. The cashier moves food across a machine called a scanner. The scanner sends a beam of light across a pattern of bars that are printed on each item. The bars form a code that tells what the item is and how much it costs.

Hospital workers use technology. There are many different kinds of machines in a hospital room. One machine helps people breathe. Another machine measures a person's heartbeat. Then it shows the information on a screen.

Police officers use technology. This police officer just wrote a parking ticket. Now she is using a tiny computer to get information about the owner of the car.

1. Why is technology important to a patient in a hospital?

2. What examples of technology do you see in your school?

LESSON 4

A NEW KIND OF NEIGHBORHOOD

This picture shows a new kind of neighborhood. The neighborhood is far above Earth. It is in outer space.

This neighborhood is called the International Space Station. Astronauts will live and work in the space station. An astronaut is a person who goes to outer space.

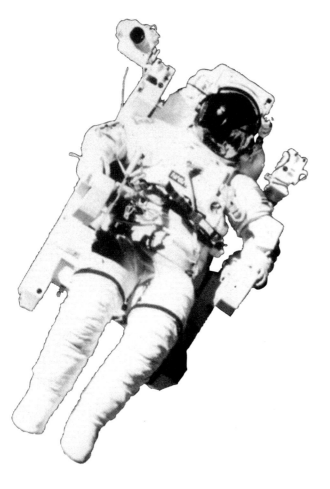

Sixteen different countries are helping to build the International Space Station. These countries include the United States of America, Russia, and Japan. People from all over the world will use the International Space Station. A community is a group of people who live in the same place. The International Space Station will be a community of people from many different countries.

This is how a laboratory on the International Space Station will look. A **laboratory** is a place where people do scientific work. Astronauts will study outer space here. They will also study how being in space affects humans and other living things.

This is what the astronauts' home in the space station will look like. The top level has a gym. The middle level has machines that control things like the air and the temperature. It is also where the astronauts will sleep. They will sleep in sleeping bags attached to the wall. The bottom level is where the astronauts will eat and relax.

1. What will astronauts do on the International Space Station?

2. Would you like to live on the space station? Why or why not?

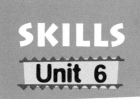

Reading a Diagram

You have seen many pictures in this book. The picture on the next page is a special kind of picture. It is a diagram. A diagram is a picture that shows you the parts of something. It also tells you what the parts are called.

This diagram shows an astronaut's space suit. The suit protects the astronaut in outer space.

1 What is the name for the part of the space suit that protects the astronaut's hand?

2 It is very cold in space, and there is no air. How does a space suit protect the astronaut from these conditions?

3 Why do you think the astronaut has a TV camera on her helmet?

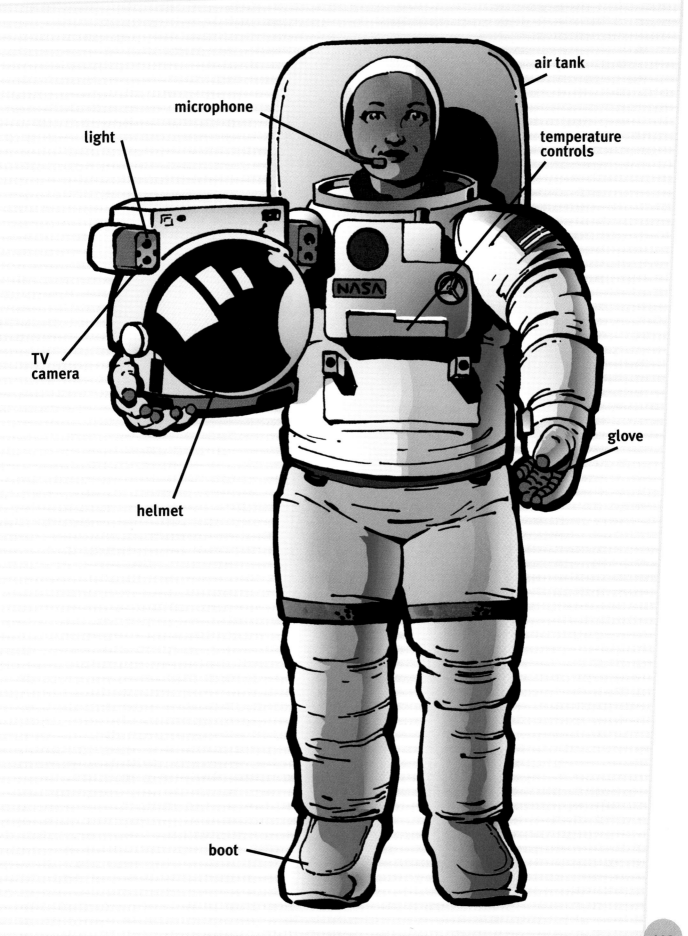

air tank

microphone

temperature
controls

light

TV
camera

glove

helmet

boot

143

Word Wrap

Use these words to complete the sentences.

technology   communication   astronaut   community laboratory

1 A _____ is a place where people do scientific work.

2 Sharing thoughts and ideas is called _____.

3 _____ is the science of machines.

4 An _____ is someone who goes into outer space.

5 A group of people living in the same place is called a _____.

Unit Wrap

The people in your neighborhood use technology every day. Technology is always changing. Thirty years ago, VCRs and cable television did not exist. Ten years ago, there were no cellular phones. In the future, people from different countries will live in a space station high above Earth.

1. **Name three ways technology helps people in your neighborhood.**

2. **Imagine your home ten years from now. What new technology do you think you will have in it?**

REVIEW SKILLS

Finding Distance on a Map

One way to measure distance in a city is to count blocks.

A block is the distance from one street to the next.

The city of Finchley has just built a new People Mover.
This map shows the People Mover's route.

1 How many blocks is it from Stop #2 to Stop #3?

2 How far is it from the Library to Stop #3?

3 Which stop is closest to the mall?

4 How many blocks long is the People Mover's route?

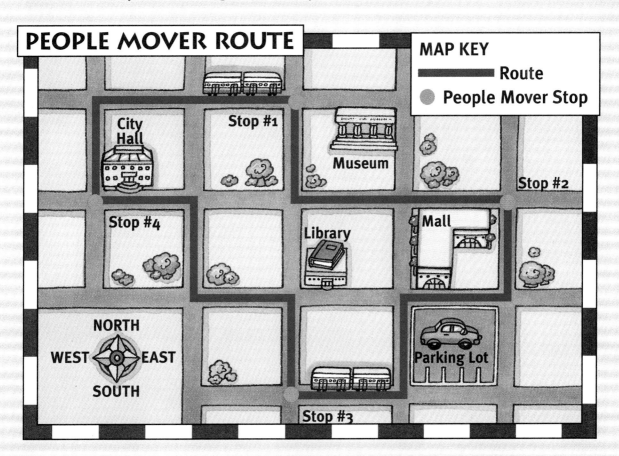

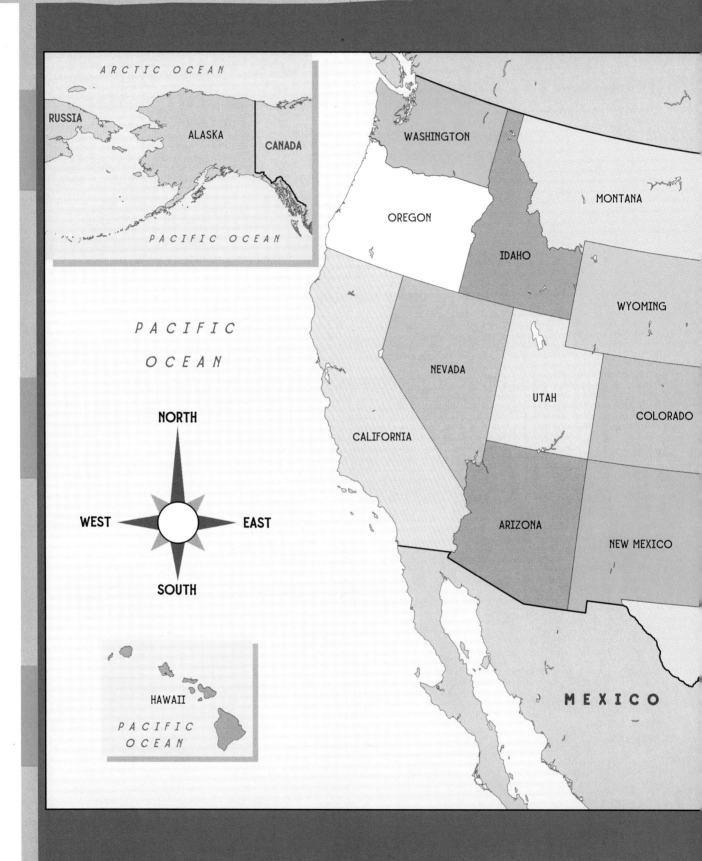

ARCTIC OCEAN

RUSSIA

ALASKA

CANADA

PACIFIC OCEAN

PACIFIC

OCEAN

NORTH

WEST — EAST

SOUTH

HAWAII

PACIFIC
OCEAN

WASHINGTON

OREGON

IDAHO

MONTANA

WYOMING

NEVADA

UTAH

COLORADO

CALIFORNIA

ARIZONA

NEW MEXICO

MEXICO

CANADA

Lake Superior

MAINE

NORTH DAKOTA

MINNESOTA

VERMONT

NEW HAMPSHIRE

Lake Huron

SOUTH DAKOTA

WISCONSIN

Lake Ontario

NEW YORK

MASSACHUSETTS

RHODE ISLAND

CONNECTICUT

Lake Michigan

MICHIGAN

Lake Erie

NEBRASKA

IOWA

INDIANA

OHIO

PENNSYLVANIA

NEW JERSEY

Washington, D. C. ★

DELAWARE

ILLINOIS

MARYLAND

WEST VIRGINIA

KANSAS

MISSOURI

VIRGINIA

KENTUCKY

NORTH CAROLINA

OKLAHOMA

ARKANSAS

TENNESSEE

SOUTH CAROLINA

MISSISSIPPI

GEORGIA

TEXAS

ALABAMA

LOUISIANA

ATLANTIC

OCEAN

FLORIDA

★ National capital

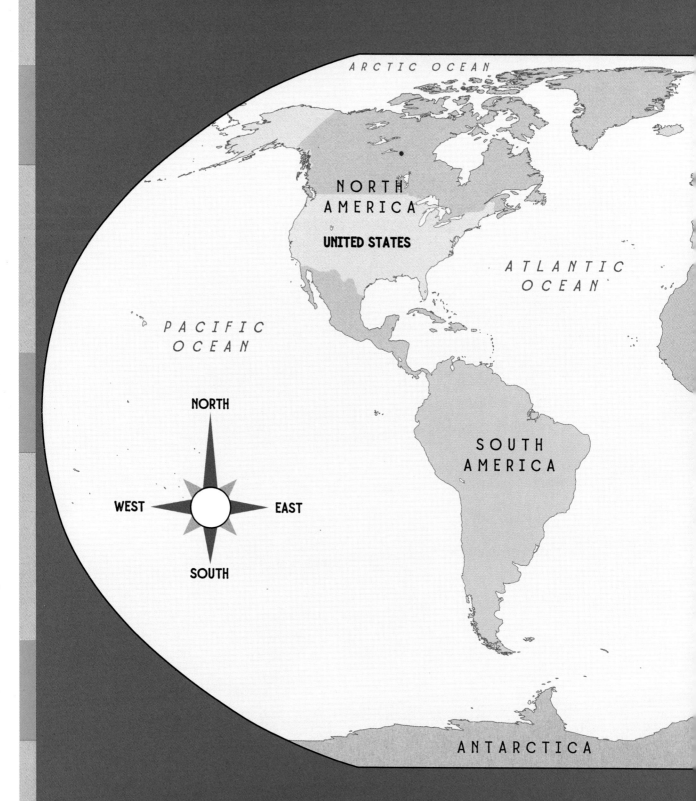

ARCTIC OCEAN

NORTH
AMERICA

UNITED STATES

ATLANTIC
OCEAN

PACIFIC
OCEAN

NORTH

WEST ⊕ EAST

SOUTH

SOUTH
AMERICA

ANTARCTICA

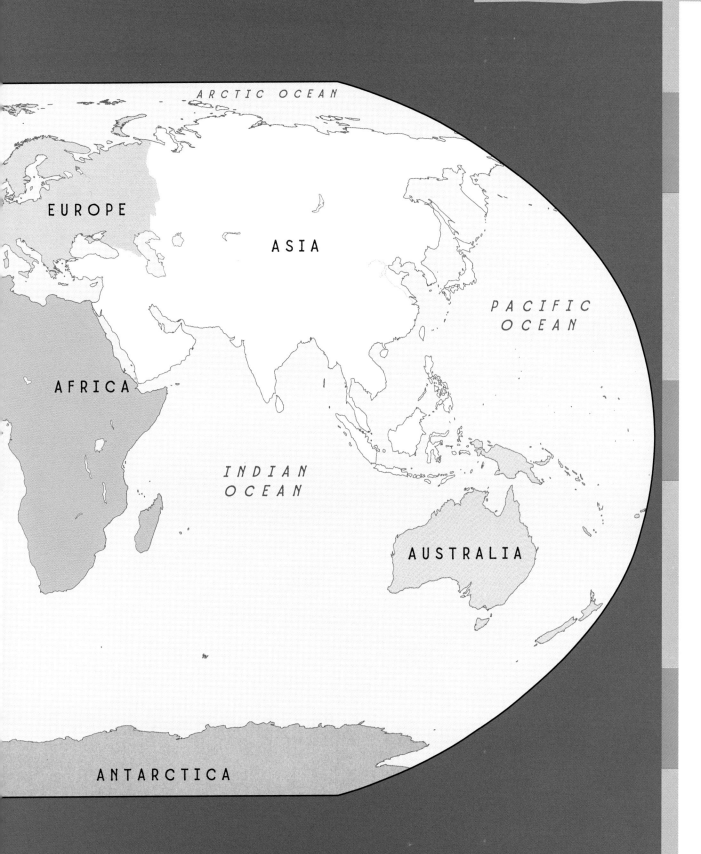

ARCTIC OCEAN

EUROPE

ASIA

PACIFIC OCEAN

AFRICA

INDIAN OCEAN

AUSTRALIA

ANTARCTICA

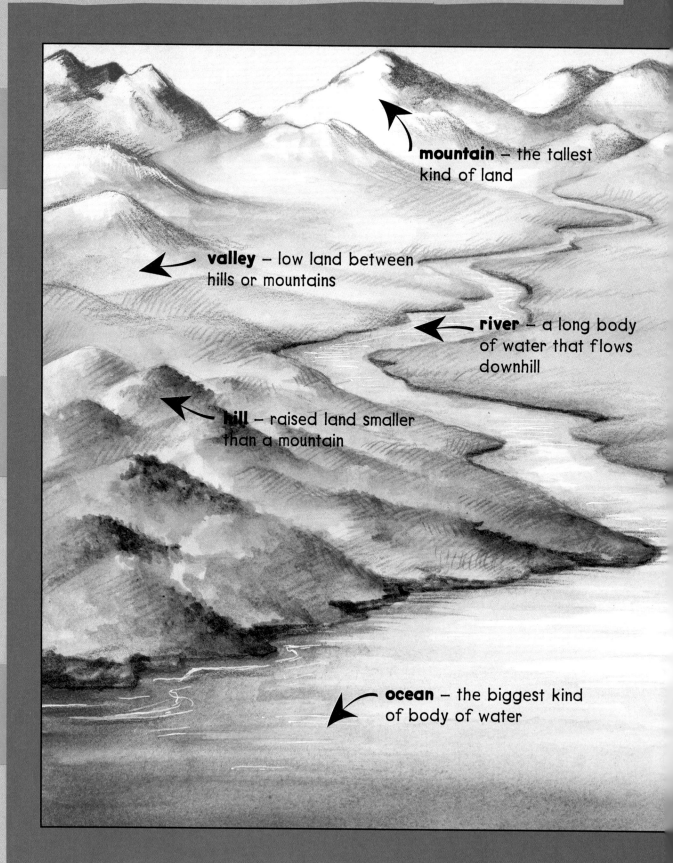

mountain – the tallest kind of land

valley – low land between hills or mountains

river – a long body of water that flows downhill

hill – raised land smaller than a mountain

ocean – the biggest kind of body of water

plain – flat land

lake – water that has land all around it

island – a piece of land surrounded by water

PICTURE GLOSSARY

ANCESTORS family members who lived before you were born. *Most* ancestors *of African Americans came from Africa.*

BAR GRAPH a chart that uses bars to show "how many." *This* bar graph *shows how many books we read.*

CALENDAR a chart that shows the months, weeks, and days of the year. *I used a* calendar *to find out what today's date is.*

CAPITAL a city where leaders of a country or state work. *Washington, D.C., is the* capital *of the United States.*

CELEBRATE to mark a special occasion by doing something special. *Many people* celebrate *the new year.*

COMMUNITY people who live in the same area. *My* community *is made up of many different people.*

COMPASS ROSE a part of a map that shows north, south, east, and west. *The map reader used the* compass rose *to find north.*

COUNTRY a land in which the people share a group of laws. *The United States is our* country.

CUSTOMS the ways a group of people does things. *Having a parade on the Fourth of July is a* custom *in the United States.*

DIRECTION North, south, east, and west are directions. *In what* direction *is Mexico from the United States?*

EARTH the planet we live on. *The United States is on planet* Earth.

ENSLAVED owned and made to work without pay. *Millions of Africans were once* enslaved *in the United States.*

EXPLORER a person who travels to an unknown place. *Matthew Henson was with one of the first* explorers *to reach the North Pole.*

FLOW CHART   a chart that shows the order in which things happen. *This* flow chart *shows how a seed becomes a tree.*

GLOBE   a model of planet Earth. *Can you find the United States on the* globe?

GOODS   things that people buy and sell. *The store sells* goods *like fruits and vegetables.*

GOVERNMENT   the leaders of a state or country. *The* government *makes laws.*

GRID MAP   a drawing of a place with lines to help map readers. *The lines on the* grid map *help people find places.*

HISTORY   a story about real events that happened long ago. *I am learning about the* history *of Detroit.*

LAW   a rule that leaders make for people. *It is against the* law *to throw trash on the ground.*

MAIN IDEA   the most important idea of a story. *The* main idea *of this book is that you should help other people.*

MAP   a drawing of a place. *This* map *shows the United States.*

MAP KEY   a chart that helps people read a map. *The map shows a red box. The* map key *tells you it is a school.*

NATURAL RESOURCES   things people use that come from nature. *Water and soil are* natural resources.

NEEDS   things that people must have to live. *Food, clothing, and shelter are* needs.

NEIGHBORHOOD   an area where people work, live, and play. *My* neighborhood *has two parks.*

PRESIDENT   the leader of a group of people. *George Washington was the first* president *of the United States.*

RELATIVES people who are in your family. *I went to visit my* relatives.

SERVICE something that people do to help others. *The firefighters do a* service *by putting out fires.*

SETTLEMENT a small village; the beginning of a new town. *Many people began moving into the new* settlement.

SETTLERS people who help build a new town to live in. *The* settlers *built their houses in the new town.*

SHELTER any place where people or animals live. *An apartment building is one form of* shelter.

STATE a large area that is part of a country. *Michigan is a* state *in our country.*

SUBURB a smaller area that is near a large city. *My cousins live in a* suburb *of Detroit.*

SYMBOL something that stands for something else. *This flag is a symbol of the United States.*

TIME LINE a chart that shows when things happened. *This* time line *shows how I grew.*

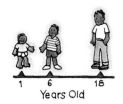

TRADE buying and selling goods. *The United States and Japan* trade *with each other.*

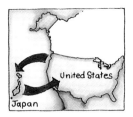

TRADITION things people do that are part of the past. *Celebrating Kwanzaa is a* tradition.

TRANSPORTATION a way of moving people and things. *A bus offers one kind of* transportation.

VOTE a way to decide or choose something. *We had a* vote *for class helper.*

WANTS things people like, but do not need. *I do not need a bicycle, but it is one of my* wants.

INDEX

CREDITS

Art Credits

Unit 4, 78–79 Donna Perrone; 86 Susan Blubaugh; Unit 5, 104–105, 121 Anne Stanley; 110–111 Susan Blubaugh; 118–119 John S. Dykes, Unit 6, 128, 133, 145 Anne Stanley; 132 John S. Dykes; 140–141 Hormoz Nabili; 142–143 Joe St. Pierre

Photo Credits

Front Cover: (top background) Index Stock Photography, (bottom background) Stephen Ogilvy, (top left inset) NASA, (top right inset) Jon Feingersh/The Stock Market, (bottom left inset) Bob Krist/The Stock Market, (center right inset) Lawrence Migdale, (bottom right inset) Gordon Alexander, (foreground) John Fortunato

Back Cover: Index Stock Photography

Title Page: John Fortunato; iii: (top left) Pinderhughes/The Stock Market, (top center) Bruce Plotkin/Tony Stone Images, (right) Gordon Alexander, (bottom left) Lawrence Migdale/Photo Researchers, Inc., (bottom center) A. Ramey/Woodfin Camp & Associates, Inc.; iv: (top) Bob Krist/The Stock Market, (left) Jay Freis/The Image Bank, (center right) Charles Thatcher/Tony Stone Images, (bottom right) Gordon Alexander, (foreground) Ross Whitaker/The Image Bank; v: (top left) Gary Buss/FPG International, (top right) Gordon Alexander, (center left) Charles Gupton/Stock Boston, (center right) Jon Feingersh/The Stock Market, (bottom left) Mark Richards/PhotoEdit, (bottom right) NASA; 72: (inset) Gordon Alexander; 72–73: (background) Wesley Bocxe/Photo Researchers, Inc.; 73: (top inset) Billy Hustace/Tony Stone Images, (center inset) Paul Chesley/Tony Stone Images, (bottom inset) Bob Daemmrich/The Image Works; 74: (left) Stephen Ogilvy, (right) Betty Press/Woodfin Camp & Associates, Inc.; 74–75: Lawrence Migdale/Photo Researchers, Inc.; 75: (top) Pinderhughes/The Stock Market; 76: (top) Lawrence Migdale/Photo Researchers, Inc., (bottom) Stephen Ogilvy; 80: (left) Gordon Alexander, (right) A. Ramey/Woodfin Camp & Associates, Inc.; 81: (background) Robert Frerck/Woodfin Camp & Associates, Inc., (inset) Corbis/Dave G. Houser; 82: Lawrence Migdale; 83: Gerald Buthaud/Woodfin Camp & Associates, Inc.; 84: Nancy Ney/The Stock Market; 84–85: Robert Essel/The Stock Market; 85: Lawrence Migdale/Photo Researchers, Inc.; 88: (left) Leland Bobbe/Tony Stone Images, (right) Gordon Alexander; 88–89: Lawrence Migdale/Tony Stone Images; 89: Bruce Plotkin/Tony Stone Images; 90: Gordon Alexander; 90–91 Barry Iverson/Woodfin Camp & Associates, Inc.; 91: Corbis/Annie Griffiths Belt; 92: Pinderhughes/The Stock Market; 94: (left inset) Stephen Ogilvy, (right inset) Stephen Ogilvy; 94–95: (background) Robert Brenner/PhotoEdit; 95: (top inset) Lawrence Migdale/Stock Boston, (center inset) Jay Freis/The Image Bank, (bottom inset) Lawrence Migdale/Photo Researchers, Inc.; 96: (all photographs) Gordon Alexander; 96–97: Gordon Alexander; 97: (top left) Rafael Macia/PhotoResearchers, Inc., (top right) Gordon Alexander; 98: Bob Krist/The Stock Market; 99: (top) Charles Thatcher/Tony Stone Images, (bottom) Ross Whitaker/The Image Bank; 100: Don Mason/The Stock Market; 101: Gordon Alexander; 102: Gordon Alexander; 103: Jens Jorgen-Jensen/The Stock Market; 106: Cheryl Naeder/Tony Stone Images; 107: (left) Tony Freeman/PhotoEdit, (right) Jacqui Hurst/Corbis; 108: Gabe Palmer/The Stock Market; 109: David Frazier/Tony Stone Images; 112: (top background & bottom background) Gordon Alexander, (inset) Mary Kate Denny/PhotoEdit; 113: (top background & bottom background) Gordon Alexander, (inset) David Young-Wolff/PhotoEdit; 114: (all background photographs) Gordon Alexander, (inset) George Haling/Photo Researchers, Inc.; 115: (top) Lifetouch National School Studios, Inc., (center & bottom) Gordon Alexander; 116: (top left) Jose Pelaez/The Stock Market, (top right & bottom) Gordon Alexander; 116–117: (bottom) Gordon Alexander; 117: (background) Gordon Alexander, (inset) Seth Resnick/Liaison International; 120: Don Mason/The Stock Market; 122: (inset) Stephen Ogilvy; 122–123: (background) Gordon Alexander; 123: (top) Mauro Fermeriello/Photo Researchers, Inc., (center) Tony Freeman/PhotoEdit, (bottom) Jon Feingersh/The Stock Market; 124: Paul Barton/The Stock Market; 125: Gary Buss/FPG International; 126: José L. Pelaez/The Stock Market; 127: Jon Feingersh/The Stock Market; 129: Aaron Haupt/Photo Researchers, Inc.; 130: William Taufic/The Stock Market; 130–131: (background) Gordon Alexander; 131: (inset) Gordon Alexander; 134: (top) Mark Richards/PhotoEdit, (bottom) Peter Beck/The Stock Market; 135: Charles Gupton/Stock Boston; 136: Pete Saloutos/The Stock Market; 137: Spencer Grant/Stock Boston; 138: NASA; 138–139: NASA; 144: Mauro Fermeriello/Photo Researchers, Inc.